HISTORY OF ROCK AND ROLL

Renaissance of Rock:
THE BRITISH INVASION

Written by: Stuart A. Kallen
Edited by: Bob Italia

Published by Abdo & Daughters, 6537 Cecilia Circle, Bloomington, Minnesota 55435

Library bound edition distributed by Rockbottom Books, Pentagon Tower, P.O. Box 36036, Minneapolis, Minnesota 55435

Library of Congress Number: 89-084917   ISBN: 0-939179-75-X

Cover Photos by: Michael Ochs Archive
Illustrations by: Michael Ochs Archive
      Bettmann Archive: pg. 38

THE BEATLES

"The British are coming, the British are coming" yelled Paul Revere as his horse galloped through the streets of Lexington, Massachusetts, during his famous midnight ride in 1775. If Paul Revere would have ridden through the streets of New York City on New Years Day, 1964, yelling the same thing, people would have thought he was very strange. But Paul Revere would have been right. Because two weeks later, on January 13, 1964, the British invaded the United States again. But this time they didn't arrive in gunboats and on horses, using rifles, to conquer America. No, this time they arrived on seven-inch, vinyl records, using guitars to conquer America. And this time, America surrendered immediately when John, Paul, George and Ringo sang "I Want to Hold Your Hand."

The Mop Tops, the Fab Four, the Lads from Liverpool, Beatlemania — new phrases had to be invented to describe them! The Beatles broke *every record ever set* in the entertainment industry, and to this day those records remain unchallenged. Overnight, the shaggy-haired Beatles, clad in pointy boots and collarless suit

*The Beatles - left: Paul McCartney; uppermiddle: George Harrison;
lowermiddle: Ringo Starr; right: John Lennon.*

coats were on the front pages of every newspaper and magazine in America. There were Beatle dolls, Beatle posters, Beatle bubblegum, Beatle bubblebath, Beatle lunchboxes, and even Beatle wigs! In 1964 alone, Americans bought $50 million worth of Beatle paraphernalia.

When the Beatles arrived in New York City on February 7, 1964, four thousand screaming fans greeted them at Kennedy Airport. After they completely charmed the reporters at their press conference an hour later, America was never the same. An epidemic of joyous insanity swept over the land as fast as the airwaves could carry it. Everywhere the Beatles went, hordes of screaming and fainting fans dogged their every step. Radio stations became obsessed with the Beatles, playing their records around the clock, making announcements like "...It's thirty-four Beatle degrees outside at nine-fifteen, Beatle time..."

IT STARTED IN LIVERPOOL

On October 9, 1940, Liverpool, England was shaking and burning, under attack from Nazi warplanes. Liverpool was a seaport town where ships were built, and the Nazis wanted it destroyed. At seven a.m., a newborn baby was crying at the Maternity Hospital on Oxford Street. The bombs rained death all over Liverpool as John Winston Lennon drew his first breath. His father, Fred, a sailor, had temporarily disappeared. His mother, Julia, wondered how she would be able to support her son. John's Aunt Mimi was beside herself with joy!

John's early life was an emotional tug of war between his mother, his father and his aunt. Julia gave John to her sister Mimi to raise. Fred Lennon would suddenly return from sea demanding custody of the boy. Julia would feel guilty and have Johnny live with her for a few months, then return him to Mimi's care. The pain of being abandoned never left John. Lennon said in later years that many of his life's problems were because of his childhood insecurity.

John was a "teddy boy" in his teen years. Teddy boys were the tough kids that greased their hair back and wore black leather jackets. All through high school, Lennon got in trouble with his teachers and his aunt. However, while Johnny showed a gruff exterior to the world, in his heart, he was a poet and an artist. The artwork he did, even when he was young, showed much promise.

The Beatles charm America at their first press conference.

LENNON MEETS McCARTNEY

When John was 16, Elvis Presley introduced Rock-n-Roll to the world. Thousands of young people in England were imitating their American cousins by picking up guitars and learning to sing. John Lennon got swept up in the new fad. Remembering that his mother played banjo, John got Julia to buy him a guitar and show him a few banjo chords.

Within months, Lennon was leading a band made up of his high school chums. On June 15, 1956, John's band was playing at church. John's friend Ivan brought along another kid to see Lennon's band. After the group was finished, Ivan's friend, Paul McCartney, met John and started showing off his musical talent. Paul played several rock songs, then did a Little Richard imitation. Lennon, being a tough guy, pretended not to notice this fourteen year old boy who was almost better than he was. But soon, destiny took its course, and the two boys were united in a band named after their school, Quarry Bank High. Lennon and McCartney's first band was called "The Quarrymen."

Paul McCartney was born June 18, 1942 to middle class parents. His childhood was much more normal than John's, and Paul was a very good natured boy who avoided trouble and worked hard in school. When Paul was fourteen, his mother, Mary, died of cancer. Paul tried to drown the sorrow of his loss by playing guitar, and by the time he met John, he was obsessed with the instrument.

AND GEORGE MAKES THREE

John and Paul were now great friends. They spent all their time together showing each other new chords on the guitar. One day, Paul brought a friend of his to meet John. Even though George Harrison was four years younger than Lennon, Paul thought George was so good that John would like him.

George Harrison was born February 25, 1943. He was the youngest Beatle and had loving, supportive parents. Even though he dressed like a teddy boy, George was quiet and shy. George's mother, Louise, encouraged him to play music. Louise would sit up with George until two o'clock in the morning, helping him practice until his fingers bled! Throughout George's career, Louise was always his biggest fan.

Because of their age difference, Lennon tried to ignore George. This was hard to do because he was hanging around the Quarrymen with increasing frequency. But George had two things working in his favor that helped him get in the band. His father was the school bus driver, and his mother allowed the boys to practice in the Harrison's home! Soon John, Paul and George were a trio.

JOHNNY AND THE MOONDOGS

As John grew older, he spent less time with his strict Aunt Mimi and more time with his mother, Julia, who lived several miles away. Just as they were rekindling their friendship and making up for lost time, Julia was run over by a bus and killed. After that tragedy, John's personality took a turn for the worse. John had always been sarcastic, but now he insulted people, shoplifted, drank alcohol, drew obscene pictures and made a general nuisance of himself at college. John's eyesight was very bad, but he refused to wear glasses, so he lost many of the fights he picked.

As a band, John, Paul and George kept getting better. In that first year, Lennon and McCartney wrote about one hundred songs together, including the early Beatle's hit, "Love Me Do." The band didn't have a regular group of players, and the boys would play with whoever showed up at their gigs. They settled on the name Johnny and the Moondogs and recruited one of Johnny's friends, Stu Sutcliffe, to play bass guitar. Stu was an artist who had never played music in his life, but after a few instructions from John and Paul, he was a bass player!

THE SILVER BEATLES

In 1959, the group had an important audition, and they needed a new name. Since the band played the music of Buddy Holly and the Crickets, they tried to think of a name like "The Crickets." John thought of "The Beetles," but changed the spelling to give it a "BEAT." And so the Beatles became a reality. To add sparkle to the name, they called themselves "The Silver Beatles" for about a year.

HAMBURG

By the time 1960 rolled around, the Beatles had added a drummer named Pete Best to their line-up. They were playing regularly at a Liverpool club called "The Cavern" and they had quite a following. The Cavern was an abandoned wine cellar turned music club. When the Beatles packed 350 people into the place during their lunchtime show, the music could not be heard above the screams of girls.

While working in the Cavern, the Beatles met a music promoter who offered them a job in Hamburg, Germany. The Beatles lept at the offer, and even though George was only seventeen, soon the Beatles were on their way to Germany.

The Beatles had been tough guys on their home turf, but they had never seen anything like Hamburg, Germany. Hamburg, like Liverpool, was a seaport town, but there the similarity ended. Gangsters ran the town, and Hamburg had the reputation of being the "sin city" of Europe.

When playing in the German clubs, the Beatles were expected to play shows lasting eight hours.

Lacking the material to fill up so much time, they started improvising, jamming songs for twenty minutes at a time. The clubs were so wild that fights would break out, people would swing from the rafters, throw things and jump off tables into the crowd. John Lennon might show up wearing a toilet seat around his neck and one night the band fell through the stage onto the floor below! In the middle of all this chaos, the Beatles were honing their skills, getting drunk, insulting the audience and generally having a great time. After five successful months, it was discovered that George was only seventeen, and not old enough to be in a bar, so the Beatles were forced to return to Liverpool.

THE LONG AND WINDING ROAD

Having spent all their money in Hamburg, the Beatles returned home penniless. After having the best professional experience ever, their spirits were broken when they were forced to return to Liverpool. But after working odd jobs for a few months, the Beatles were ready to perform again.

On December 27, 1960, the Beatles played their

first post-Hamburg concert. The ruckus created at the Litherland Town Hall showed the Beatles the way of the future. Dressed in leather pants, cowboy boots and scruffy, long hair, the Beatles' wild music and new songs caused a riot that night in Liverpool. All those hours on stage in Hamburg had finally paid off. Word spread around Liverpool — the Beatles were the next big thing! Beatle concerts turned into riots everywhere they played, and by 1961 the group was ready to return to Hamburg.

When they did, the Beatles were treated as stars. Stu Sutcliffe's girlfriend, Astrid, cut the Beatles' hair, giving them bangs and leaving the rest long and shaggy. Astrid also made them suit coats without collars. While in Germany, the Beatles made their first record, backing a singer named Tony Sheridan on a song called "My Bonnie." After their engagement in Germany was over, Stu decided to quit the Beatles and marry Astrid. Paul was then made the Beatles left-handed bass player.

In April of 1962, Stu started having violent headaches, and two weeks later, he was dead from a brain hemmorrhage. A year earlier, Sutcliffe had been severly beaten up in Hamburg, and the damage the beating had done to his head was blamed for the cause of his death.

14

WHO ARE THE BEATLES?

In the Nems Record Store in Liverpool, Brian Epstein, the store's owner, was frustrated. People had been coming into the store asking for a record called "My Bonnie" by a group called the Beatles. Brian hadn't heard of the record or the band. "Who are the Beatles?" Brian asked his record distributers. No one knew. When Brian found out that the Beatles were playing at The Cavern the next day, he decided to check them out.

"It was black, as a deep grave, dark, dank and smelly," said Brian about The Cavern, "but something about the band intrigued me."

Within weeks, Brian had signed on as the Beatles' manager. He had never managed a band before, but he had some contacts in the record business through his record shop. Brian put the Beatles in suits and ties and made them clean up their stage act. No more smoking on stage and eating between songs. Brian told the Beatles they were going to be the biggest group ever.

Epstein set about getting the Beatles a solid line-up of engagements. But playing Liverpool and Hamburg was not a way to be the biggest group ever. Brian took tapes down to London, but the

Beatles were rejected by every single record company Epstein approached. No one wanted a group from Liverpool. And besides, "groups with guitars are on their way out." After several disappointing months, George Martin, a producer at EMI, gave the Beatles a listen. The Beatles had already been rejected by EMI, but his company was so big that Martin didn't know.!

PETE'S OUT, RINGO'S IN

George Martin liked the Beatles and wanted to sign them on Parlophone Records. There was only one problem. Martin didn't think the Beatles drummer, Pete Best, was good enough. Pete had to go. Pete was well loved by the loyal Beatle fans and people protested at The Cavern carrying signs that said "Pete forever, Ringo never." The other three Beatles agreed with Martin, and soon the unlucky Best was gone. The job was given to a drummer who wore two rings on each hand, Ringo Starr.

Richard Starkey (Ringo) is the oldest of the Beatles. He too was born while Liverpool was being bombed, on July 7, 1940. Ringo was a sickly child and was in and out of hospitals for most of his young life.

When Ringo was twenty, he was offered a job playing drums with the biggest group in Liverpool, Rory Storme and the Hurricanes. Because drum kits were so expensive and hard to carry around, drummers in Liverpool were in short supply. Ringo had as many as four bands bidding for his services. Ringo joined the Beatles simply because they offered him the most money.

With the addition of Ringo, the Beatles became the most popular group in Liverpool. Girls knocked on Aunt Mimi's door asking for John. Paul and George were chased down the streets by mobs of screaming teenage girls. Ringo met his future wife, Maureen, when she walked up to him and boldly kissed him as he headed for the stage at The Cavern. There was no publicity or hype causing all this hysteria, just John, Paul, George and Ringo playing music the only way they knew how.

BEATLEMANIA

October 16, 1963, marks the beginning of the worldwide phenomenon known as "Beatlemania." That was the night 15 million people in England

The Fab Four are awarded by the Royal family.

turned on their televisions and saw the Beatles singing "She Loves You." Beatlemania spread like wildfire across the globe. Long hair was suddenly acceptable on men for the first time in a hundred years!

The Beatles' February '64 tour of America was a national spectacle never to be repeated. The nation, still reeling from the assassination of President John Kennedy, was in need of something to cheer it up. And the Beatles, with their charming wit and great music, fit the bill nicely. 60,000 ticket requests for the Beatles' appearance on the Ed Sullivan Show had to be refused. (Elvis only received 7,000 requests.) For the first time *stadiums* were being filled for Rock-n-Roll concerts. Sadly, the Beatles became prisoners to their fame. The screaming at the concerts drowned out the music. Hotels where they stayed were mobbed by thousands of girls. If any of the Beatles were seen on the streets, they would be attacked by people who tried to rip off their clothes and grab handfuls of their hair.

By April 4, 1964, the Beatles were on top of the charts and on top of the world. The following is a list of records the Beatles set that remain unchallenged to this day. With the release of "Can't Buy Me Love," the Beatles:

. Held the first five postions on the Top 100.
. Had ten singles on the Top 100.
. Entered "Can't Buy Me Love" on the charts at Number 1, a first.
. Had the most Number 1 singles in a row.
. Had 2,100,000 orders for "Can't Buy Me Love" before the single was released.

IT'S BEEN A HARD DAY'S NIGHT

The streets were closed around the London Pavillion on July 6, 1964. Thousands of Beatlemaniacs were pushed behind police barricades in Picadilly Circus. One by one the Rolls-Royces arrived, carrying the Fab Four and other less famous people such as Princess Margaret. The occasion was the world premier of "A Hard Day's Night."

The Beatles' first movie won the hearts of even their worst critics. It also proved that the Beatles were here to stay. Filmed for a mere half a million dollars, the movie recreates a day in the life of the Beatles. The movie, directed by Richard Lester, was planned by United Artists before the Beatles were famous outside of England. By the time the movie was released, the Beatles were huge stars, and 15,000 copies of the movie had to be printed, setting yet another record.

The Beatles first movie "A Hard Day's Night" is a smash.

Full of clever jokes, new "hip" words, and great songs, "Hard Day's Night" was filmed in a style that is now used by almost everybody on MTV. Through the use of quick scene changes and strange camera angles, the Beatles became pioneers in the film industry as well as the recording industry.

HELP!

While fans were grabbing up anything with the word "Beatles" on it, the Beatles themselves were working as hard as a band could work. Touring the world, returning to England, going straight to the studio to make records, touring England, back to America, more recording, another movie, this one was appropriately entitled "Help." John, Paul, George and Ringo kept up this breakneck pace until 1966.

"Help" received far less praise than "Hard Day's Night" but the fans didn't care. They were just thrilled to see their heroes on the silver screen. The Beatles, tired of all the pandemonium of touring, checked into Abby Road Studios in London and began work on their next album,

At New York's Shea Stadium the Beatles play to a sold out crowd. Even the self assured Lennon was shocked by the crowds admiration.

Rubber Soul. It was to be the sixth Beatle album in three years! For the first time the Beatles were in control in the recording studio, and the folk-rock influence of Bob Dylan can be clearly heard on the album. Once again, the Beatles had a million seller on their hands, and thousands of bands were falling over themselves to find the folk-rock sound.

CONTROVERSY

Controversy came when John Lennon, in a discussion about religion, said that "the Beatles were more popular than Jesus." The remark, taken out of context, passed unnoticed in England. But when the American news service picked it up, there was a severe Beatle backlash. In the South, disc jockeys were painting John Lennon as Satan and urged people to burn their Beatle records. There were anti-Beatle rallies, public record burnings and Ku Klux Klan demonstrators outside Beatle concerts. Lennon apologized, but he was very shaken, and on August 29, 1966, though no one knew it, the Beatles played their last live concert in San Francisco. The world was changing and the

The Fab Four looking bored and frustrated in their hotel room while on their American tour.

Beatles were changing with it. The intricate music they were playing in the studio could not be reproduced in front of 60,000 screaming teenagers. And while the Beatles were liberating the world, they themselves were prisoners in hotels and windowless recording studios day and night. It was time for a change.

WE ALL LIVE IN A YELLOW SUBMARINE

While the Beatles were playing their last concert, the vinyl presses at EMI were running at full speed. Once again, the Beatles were about to bowl over anybody trying to second guess what they were up to. The new album, "Revolver," would show the world that the Beatles could do more than write catchy love songs. Included on "Revolver" were songs showing the Beatles' increasing interest in mysticism and philosophy. The album included everything from the London Symphony Orchestra on "Eleanor Rigby" to the sound of bubbles being blown in a glass on "Yellow Submarine" to lyrics taken from the Egyptian Book of the Dead on "Tomorrow Never Knows." Of course, the album was a huge success.

One of the Beatles many T.V. appearances.

THE SUMMER OF LOVE
AND SGT. PEPPER

In January of 1967, all was quiet in the Beatles' camp. The Beatle-hungry public was used to a constant flow of records from the boys, and rumors were flying that the Beatles were breaking up. In reality, the Beatles were once again outdoing themselves. When "Strawberry Fields Forever" and "Penny Lane" were released as a single, the world of Rock-n-Roll would never be the same.

From the opening notes of "Strawberry Fields," John Lennon takes us on a kaleidoscopic journey through his thoughts and childhood memories, creating sound environments that consist of haunting cellos and echoing drums. A new keyboard invention called the Mellotron filled in with noises never heard before by the human ear. The Beatles made short films for each song, thus inventing "music videos." The Beatles looked very serious with their newly grown mustaches and with John appearing for the first time ever in rimless spectacles. After the video appeared on The Ed Sullivan Show, mustaches and rimless glasses sprouted up on faces all over the world.

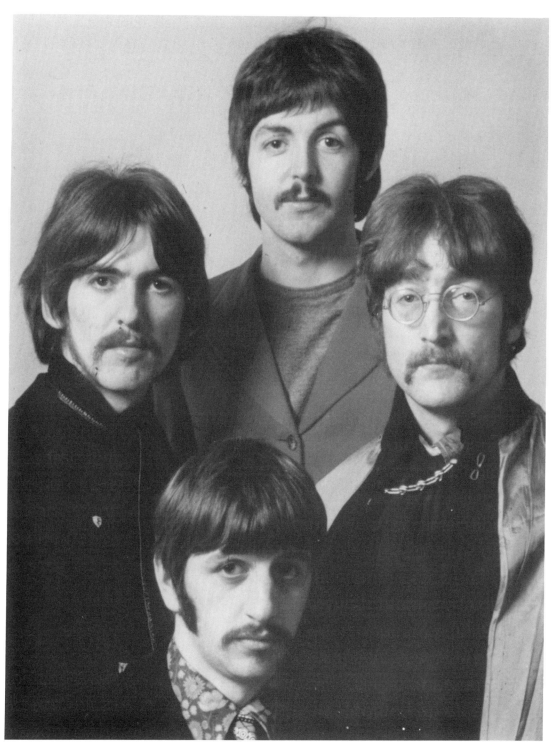

The more mature looking Beatles, weathered from years of hard work.

The Beatles were getting further and further out. Lennon had his Rolls-Royce painted with psychedelic colors and Harrison had planets and stars painted on his house. The Beatles "image" had changed beyond recognition in the span of four years. "Strawberry Fields Forever" and "Penny Lane" became the soundtrack for the "Summer of Love" that was just beginning in San Francisco. It seemed the joy and creativity would never end.

IT WAS TWENTY YEARS AGO TODAY

What was the first record to have a fold out cover, all the words to the songs printed on it, and a paper insert with cut-outs? The same album that, to this very day, is considered by critics and listeners alike to be the most important Rock album EVER — Sgt. Pepper's Lonely Hearts Club Band. While peace marches, human be-ins and outdoor rock concerts were happening all over America, here come the Beatles—dressed in old-fashion, silk marching band uniforms!

"Sgt. Pepper" inspired bands like The Who and The Rolling Stones to make their own "Sgt. Pepper" type albums. Until the cost cutting measures of the late 70s, "concept albums" with the words printed on the cover were standard Rock-n-Roll practices.

After "Sgt. Pepper," the Beatles were invited to play on the *first worldwide,* satellite television broadcast. The Beatles were asked to write a song with words simple enough to be understood by people who didn't speak much English. On June 25, 1967, the Beatles sang "All You Need Is Love" to *one-hundred and fifty million people* all over the world.

ROLL UP FOR THE MYSTERY TOUR

Although only in their mid-twenties, the Beatles had all the money, glory and power that a Rock-n-Roll band could ever hope for. But they still thought something was missing. Their search for a higher truth led them to India, where they began to meditate with a guru named Maharishi Mahesh Yogi. Suddenly the bearded guru was a superstar, and thousands of people headed to India to find enlightenment.

While the Beatles were in Wales meditating with Maharishi, their manager, Brian Epstein, died.

Brian was very depressed when the Beatles stopped playing concerts. Epstein felt that the Beatles didn't need his services any more and started taking sleeping pills in mass quantities. This led to his death on August 27, 1967. Now the Beatles were on their own business-wise, and it was a long downhill slide for their financial well-being.

Paul pulled the band together and decided to make a movie. Although none of the Beatles were actual film makers, they all boarded a pschedelically painted bus filled with actors and friends and headed off into the English countryside to make "Magical Mystery Tour." The resulting hour long film was shown to fifteen million Britons on December 26, 1967, and the Beatles were faced with the first bomb of their professional careers.

The English press declared "Mystery Tour" to be "rubbish," and plans for an American release were scrapped. This was the beginning of the split between Paul and the rest of the Beatles. Not surprisingly, the album "Magical Mystery Tour" was much more successful than the movie, and once again John Lennon amazed the world, this time with "I am the Walrus."

TAKING A BITE OF THE APPLE

As the year 1967 wound to a close, it seemed the whole world was high on peace and love. The starry-eyed Beatles were meditating with their guru in India and, far from the distractions of the world, they wrote thirty songs. Reality however, was about to rear its head. The Maharishi made sexual advances on several of the women who were traveling with the Beatles. Disappointed and disillusioned, the Beatles returned to England from the last trip they would ever take together.

Once they were back in London, the Beatles decided to use their massive wealth and power to start their own record and movie company. According to the Beatles, for the first time, the younger generation would be able to create without having to ask "the men in suits" for money. Apple Corps. was born, and the Beatles ran full page ads in newspapers asking for tapes and ideas from unknown artists.

Apple was swamped with tapes and scripts and off the wall proposals. People descended on their offices like vultures. Groups of Hell's Angels and hippies moved into Apple's offices, and no one wanted to be "unhip" and ask them to leave.

Hundreds of people were on the Apple payroll, but they did nothing more than party all day. Anything that wasn't nailed down was carried away.

Despite all the mayhem, the first single released on the Apple label, "Hey Jude" / "Revolution" became the largest selling Beatle single of all time.

While all this madness was going on, a cartoon entitled "Yellow Submarine" was released. Like everything else that the Beatles touched, the cartoon was a first. Created from over five million drawings, German artist Heinz Edelmann pieced together a fantasy story of color and magic. The Beatles added four new songs to the cartoon and once again the world was astounded.

OH YOKO

When John Lennon attended the premier of "Yellow Submarine," his wife Cynthia, whom he married in 1962, was not with him. John had a different escort that night, and it was a woman who, with John, would stir up controversy all over the world in the next few years.

John had met Yoko Ono at an art gallery in 1967, and was very impressed with her abstract artwork.

The Fab Four show off their success.

One night after making experimental recordings with Yoko, John realized he was in love with her. John felt Yoko was much more in tune with his artistic concepts than Cynthia. Soon John and Cynthia were divorced.

Yoko and John became inseparable. When Yoko attended the Beatles recording sessions, Paul, George and Ringo became upset. The studio had always been off limits to wives and girlfriends. This jealousy caused tension between John and the rest of the band.

THE WHITE ALBUM

Soon after John met Yoko, the Beatles released another album. This one, a double record set (the first rock album with two records in one sleeve) was simply entitled "The Beatles." The album included a poster with all the song lyrics and photos of the four Beatles. Because of the albums' stark white cover, it became known as "The White Album."

"The White Album" showed the Beatles getting back to basics. Instead of crashing orchestras, the Beatles were once again utilizing vocals, guitars and drums. "The White Album" is a potpourri of musical styles — old time swing music like "Honey Pie," Beach Boy style like "Back in the U.S.S.R.," weird sound experiments like Lennon's "Revolution 9," and acoustic goodies like "Rocky Raccoon."

But the Beatles weren't working as a unit anymore. Each member of the band did their own songs, without the group input of the early days. John would lay down a couple of tracks, and Paul would come in days later and put on the bass track. Ringo would get mad at Paul's bossiness and leave in frustration, only to come back to find that Paul had done the drums himself. In short, the Beatles were falling apart.

WHO CAN FILL BRIAN'S SHOES?

By now, the Beatles were losing $40,000 a week at Apple. (That's like losing over a half million by today's standards.) All the people they had hired were eating and drinking away the Beatles' money at an alarming rate. The Beatles decided they needed a tough new manager to get their business affairs in line so they could get on with the job of playing music. Enter into the picture Allen Klein.

John and Yoko.

Klein was a wheeler dealer from New York, and the manager of the Rolling Stones. John, George and Ringo liked Klein, but Paul wanted Lee Eastman to control Apple. Eastman is Linda McCartney's father. (She and Paul were married March 12, 1969.)

While lawyers and managers fought over the Beatles' empire, John and Yoko held media events to further the cause of world peace. After they were married in Gibraltar on March 20, 1969, John and Yoko invited the world press to attend their honeymoon, which John dubbed "a bed-in for world peace." John and Yoko simply sat in bed wearing white pajamas while T.V. cameras whirred and reporters shook their heads.

The Lennon's continued traveling around the world, protesting "all the suffering and violence in the world." In Montreal, John invited celebrities up to his hotel room, recorded a song he wrote called "Give Peace a Chance," and released the single the next day. That song has become an anthem for peace movements everywhere.

COME TOGETHER

While John and Yoko were making front page news all over the world, Paul McCartney was urging the Beatles to return to the studio. Named after the street where the Beatles had recorded all their records for EMI, "Abby Road" turned out to be the last Beatle album. In a matter of weeks, the Beatles knocked out a musical extravaganza that rekindled the flame of the Beatles' magic.

PAUL IS DEAD

The evidence seemed conclusive. At the end of "Strawberry Fields" John says, "I buried Paul." On the Sgt. Pepper album McCartney has a patch sewn on his uniform that says, "O.P.D.," meaning "Officially Pronounced Dead." "Revolution 9" when played backwards sounds like "Turn me on, dead man." At the end of "I'm So Tried," John mutters, "Paul is a dead man, miss him, miss him."

All these clues and more started what must be one of the most bizarre rumors in show business. After a disc jockey in Michigan revealed all these so-called proofs that Paul McCartney was dead, the rumor spread like wildfire. The story went that on a "Stupid bloody Tuesday" ("I am the Walrus"), Paul had "blown his mind out in a car" ("A Day in the Life"), was "Officially Pronounced Dead" on "Wednesday morning at five o'clock" ("She's Leaving Home"). John, George and Ringo, the story went, had a McCartney look alike contest to find a replacement for Paul. Television shows and newspaper articles ran stories with all the evidence proving Paul's death.

Thousands of sobbing fans jammed the switchboard at Apple. McCartney was nowhere to be seen. When he finally emerged from his farm in Scotland and told the world, "Rumors of my death have been greatly exaggerated," many fans still believed that the Beatles "buried Paul" as some kind of huge practical joke. Lennon strongly denied any involvement, although the rumors certainly didn't hurt record sales.

THE DREAM IS OVER

By 1970, the only time the Beatles ever saw each other was to argue over money. John, Paul, George and Ringo were involved with other projects, none having to do with the Beatles. John wanted to break up the band, but Allen Klein and

McCartney, agreeing on something for once, talked him out of it.

"Get Back" was retitled "Let It Be," and the tapes were given to Phil Spector to be produced. The movie was released, disappointing most Beatlemaniacs when they saw their heroes looking bored or arguing with one another. A noon-time concert on the roof of the studio was the highlight of the movie. After the police arrived to stop the concert, the Beatles would never play in front of an audience again. On April 10, 1970, Paul McCartney announced he was leaving the Beatles, and the greatest rock group in history came crashing to an end.

AND IN THE END . . .

The Beatles changed the entire music business, turning it into the multi-billion dollar industry it is today. Beatle records and CD's still sell by the millions, and their music can be heard on radio stations around the world. All of their movies have been released on video cassette and are in constant demand by the Beatle hungry public.

John Lennon was gunned down in front of his apartment building in New York City on December 8, 1980. Marc David Chapman,

Lennon's killer, was another person who thought he heard weird messages in Beatles' songs that weren't there. John Lennon used his popularity to further the cause of world peace and justice. He was scorned at the time, but many of the issues he brought before the public started mass movements that are still going strong. Lennon helped end the Viet Nam war and started the women's equality movement. Ironically, one of John's last contributions was to buy bullet proof vests for the New York City Police Department. Unfortunatly he wasn't wearing one himself on that December night.

George, Paul and Ringo are still making records, and talk of a reunion comes up constantly in the press. And believe it or not, the lawsuits that started with the Beatles break-up in 1970 are *still* being fought in British and American courtrooms! Without John, the Beatles could never reunite, but the fact that people still wish for a reunion proves how greatly the Beatles have touched their lives. The world will always be a more colorful and musical place to live, thanks to the four young men from Liverpool: John, Paul, George and Ringo — The Beatles!

THE BRITISH INVASION

The Beatles, of course, weren't the only pop group to come out of England, but they paved the way for scores of other bands that flourished in the sixties. Groups like The Yardbirds and Cream were influenced by American blues artists such as Muddy Waters and Bo Diddley — musicians most white Americans had never heard of. Time and space does not allow a complete listing of all the great English bands, but a trip to the record store or library would reveal a wealth of great music to the curious listener.

THE ROLLING STONES —
THE BAD BOYS OF ROCK

There was nothing to do in the hotel room in Clearwater, Florida. The nervous guitar player couldn't sleep. He picked up the guitar lying on the bed, and played a riff. Using "Dancing in the Street" by Martha and the Vandallas as inspiration, Keith Richards, guitarist for the Rolling Stones, recorded the lick on his tape deck. When Mick Jagger, the group's lead singer, came in the room, he put some words to the notes, "I can't get no satisfaction." Keith thought the song was alright, but it wasn't good enough to be a hit.

The bad boys of rock - The Rolling Stones.

After the Stones recorded it at Chess Studio in Chicago, Keith still thought "Satisfaction" was a throw away. Three months later, "Satisfaction" put the Rolling Stones at number one on the charts, a place they would return to again and again.

While the Beatles were charming young and old alike with their cute moptops and clever songs, a band emerged out of the London Blues scene that was the total opposite of the Beatles. Mick Jagger and Keith Richards joined up with Brian Jones, Charlie Watts and Bill Wyman to play brash Rhythm and Blues music. The Rolling Stones, following in the tradition of the great Bluesmen, played music with a soul and an urgency that was unheard of on Top 40 radio in 1965.

KINGS OF RAUNCH AND ROLL

"Paint It Black," "Heart of Stone," "Get Off of My Cloud." As these song titles suggest, the Stones didn't sound like very nice guys. While the Beatles were saying "I Wanna Hold Your Hand," the Stones were yelling "Hey! You! Get off of my cloud!"

By 1967, the Stones had offended most of the British ruling class and a few radio programmers. They were banned from the Royal Albert Hall in London after screaming girls rushed the stage. A riot ensued only three minutes after the Stones took the stage. In America, their blatantly sexual lyrics kept the Stones' records off of many radio stations. But there was no turning back. The public wanted the Rolling Stones. Because of the Stones' vast popularity, Top 40 radio was opened up to a new style some people called "Raunch and Roll."

2000 LIGHT YEARS FROM HOME

When the Beatles released "Sgt. Pepper," the Stones jumped on the Sgt. Pepper bandwagon and released "Their Satanic Majesty's Request." The album, complete with a 3-D picture on the front, was full of meandering "cosmic" fluff, and was panned by audiences and critics alike. The Stones retreated to the studio and got back to the business of playing Rock-n-Roll.

Inspired by the student demonstrations that were happening in America and Europe, the Stones released "Beggars Banquet" in 1968. With songs

A London T.V. appearance.

like "Street Fightin Man" and "Sympathy For the Devil," "Beggars Banquet" showcased the Stones hard-hitting Rock and put them back at the top.

LET IT BLEED

The Stones didn't have a number one hit from "Beggars Banquet," and "the greatest rock and roll band in the world" was finding its pockets empty. In 1969, the Stones decided to do their first American tour in three years. Unfortunately, Brian Jones would not be accompanying the Stones on this tour. He was found dead in his swimming pool on July 3, 1969, another victim of barbituates and alcohol.

Using B.B. King and Ike and Tina Turner for warm up acts, the Rolling Stones took their Rock-n-Roll circus to Madison Square Garden in the summer of '69, as "Honky Tonk Women" was topping the charts. The Stones had just released "Let It Bleed" and they were at the peak of their raunchy power, playing songs like "Monkey Man" and "Midnight Rambler."

PLEASED TO MEET YOU,
HOPE YOU GUESS MY NAME

The tickets to the Rolling Stones concerts were $7.50 each. This price was considered outrageous at a time when a full tank of gas cost $3.00. To try to prove that they weren't greedy, the Stones decided to play a free concert in the San Francisco area — at Altamont Raceway on December 6. The show would feature the Grateful Dead, Santana, the Jefferson Airplane and of course, the Rolling Stones.

Instead of using police for concert security, the Stones decided to use the Hell's Angels Motorcycle Club. It was a sad end to the 60s. All the hopes of peace, love and music were shattered that day as the Hell's Angels, out of their minds on drugs and alcohol, beat up the concert goers with pool cues and pipes. A black man named Meredith Hunter was viciously stabbed to death by the Hell's Angels as horrified concert goers watched. This shocking event is detailed in the movie "Gimme Shelter."

A wild bunch - The Stones.

STILL GOING STRONG

As the new decade dawned, the Stones continued to knock out hit after hit. "Brown Sugar," "Angie" and "Miss You" all reached number one. In the 70s the Stones released an incredible 18 albums. As the Stones grew older, they toned down their images as rebels and set the standard for world-class, jet-setting Rock gods.

Even though Mick Jagger once said that he'd be playing Rock-n-Roll when he was 40-years-old, the Stones' '81 concert tour broke all attendence records for live concerts. Jagger's strutting bravado, backed by the Stones raunchy rhythm section, still packs stadiums and concert halls. As the 90s dawn, the Rolling Stones are planning their first concert tour in many years. The promoters are promising the Stones a $65 million profit! As the Rolling Stones enter into their 26th year as Rock superstars, they have truly earned the right to be called "the world's greatest Rock-n-Roll band."

The Stones grow-up but keep on rockin'.

THE WHO —
ROCK OPERATORS

"People try to put us d-d-d-down," stutters Roger Daltrey, shaking his long blond curls around the microphone. "Just because we get a-r-r-rround." Sneering out the rest of the verse, "Hope I die before I get old," Daltrey grabs the mic wire and starts whirling the microphone in a huge arc over his head. Behind Daltrey, Peter Townshend has gone into a frenzy of guitar assassination. Townshend windmills his arm around in a circle, strumming the strings once on every 360 degree sweep. Next to Townshend stands bassist John Entwistle, glaring at the audience and thumping out the bass line. Townshend takes off his guitar and starts smashing it, first on his amplifier, then on the stage. Drummer Keith Moon can take it no longer. In the middle of his psychotic pounding, he kicks over his bass drum and sends it skidding across the stage. Now, thrashing his cymbals, he sends them flying. Townshend's amp howls as his guitar neck finally snaps on the tenth smash to the stage floor. The crowd screams with appreciation as The Who exit the stage, the twisted wreckage of their instruments sacrificed to Rock-n-Roll.

The band that made guitar smashing famous started out in 1962, when Daltrey, Townshend and Entwistle formed a band called "The Detours." Although they were still in high school, Townshend's mother got the boys an audition with a talent agency. Soon the Detours were playing
R & B and Top 10 hits on the club circuit. When Townshend saw another band on T.V. called the Detours, the band changed their name to The Who.

SMASHING SUCCESS

In 1964, there was a group of people in London who called themselves "mods." Mods were into the flamboyant fashions of Carnaby Street-Polka-dot and paisley shirts with baggy sleeves, bell-bottom pants and mini-skirts. The Who were playing a mod club one night when a cocky young man approached the band and announced that he could play better than the group's drummer (name unknown). Keith Moon proved his point and then proceeded to trash the drums.

One night, The Who were playing a gig and Townshend accidentally broke his guitar neck on the low ceiling in the club. The audience barely noticed. Townshend then smashed the guitar to

The Who - still playing bingo halls.

smithereens and the audience went wild. Moon got into the spirit of things and kicked over the drums. The group got such widespread publicity from the stunt that instrument trashing became the standard ending for a Who concert.

ROCKS BAD BOYS

The Who recorded "Can't Explain" in 1965, and it reached number 8 in England. Their next single "Anyway, Anyhow, Anywhere" featured screeching feedback. The record company sent the tapes back to The Who because they thought the strange noise was a mistake! The Who stirred up controversy with their next single "My Generation" when they sang, "Hope I die before I get old."

Despite their success in England, The Who had problems. The cost of replacing their ruined instruments and fighting amongst the band members was taking its toll. The band released "I Can See For Miles," and it became their first U.S. hit. The Who went on their first American tour, warming up for Herman's Hermits, and earned a "bad boy" reputation for trashing their hotel rooms.

Pete Townshend - (front and center) of the Who. Rocks most rare and authentic genius.

The Who's popularity soared in the U.S. when the movie Monterey Pop Festival was released. Their antics on stage made them perfect for the youth rebellion that was taking place in America.

. . . SURE PLAYS A MEAN PINBALL

In 1969 The Who released a double album set entitled "Tommy." It was the first ever "Rock Opera." The album, about a deaf, dumb and blind boy who is a pinball champion, won rave reviews and made The Who superstars. For the next two years, Who concerts featured a two-hour rendition of the album "Tommy." In one of the more memorable scenes of the movie "Woodstock," The Who preformed the finale of "Tommy." Daltrey twirls the mic over his head while Townshend does scissor-leaps, smashes his guitar and throws it into the audience.

In 1975, "Tommy" was made into a movie with Daltrey in the lead role. In 1976, The Who won a spot in the Guinness Book of World Records for the loudest rock concert.

The Who - getting crazy. Pete does his famous scissors leap.

DEATH OF A DRUMMER

The Who continued to tour and record until September 7, 1978, when Keith Moon died. Moon was known far and wide for his crazy antics and partying life style. Unfortunately, that life style was responsible for his death.

In the 80s, The Who continued to play with drummer Kenny Jones. Their farewell tour in 1982 grossed over $40 million. They performed for the Live Aid concert in 1985, and there is talk of a Who reunion in the 90s.

The Who took Rock-n-Roll to its rebellious extremes while keeping their art intact. They were the first Punk Rockers, long before the term existed. Their format with a lead singer out front while the guitars and drums provide the thunder will be used by thousands of bands in the years to come. From broken guitars to Rock Opera, The Who are one-of-a-kind wizards of Rock.

Roger Daltrey, Pete Townshend, John Entwistle and Keith Moon.

FINAL NOTE

Many of the world's greatest guitar players such as Jimi Hendrix, Eric Clapton and Jimmy Page started their careers in the 60s. Because of the space given to the Beatles and the Rolling Stones, the guitar players that were the "Roots of Heavy Metal" are covered in volume five of this series, "Revolution of Rock — The 1970s."

BIBLIOGRAPHY

Bronson, Fred. *The Billboard Book of Number One Hits.* New York: Billboard Publications, 1988.

Brown, Peter and Gaines, Steven. *The Love You Make.* New York: McGraw-Hill Book Co., 1983.

Cepican, Bob and Ali, Waleed. *Yesterday . . . Came Suddenly.* New York: Arbor House, 1985.

Clifford, Mike. *The Harmony Illustrated Encyclopedia of Rock.* New York: Harmony Books, 1983.

Davies, Hunter. *The Beatles.* New York: McGraw-Hill, 1978.

Norman, Phillip. *Symphony for the Devil.* New York: Linden Press / Simon & Schuster, 1984.

Schaffner, Nicholas. *The Boys From Liverpool.* New York: Methuen, 1980.

Santelli, Robert. *Sixties Rock.* Chicago: Contemporary Books, Inc., 1985.

Stokes, Geoffrey. *The Beatles.* New York: Rolling Stone Press, 1980.

Ward, Ed and Stokes, Geoffrey and Tucker, Ken. *Rock of Ages.* New York: Rolling Stone Press / Summit Books, 1986.